MEGHAN TRAINOR

★ FAMOUS MUSIC STAR ★

Big Buddy Books

An Imprint of Abdo Publishing
abdopublishing.com

BIG BUDDY POP BIOGRAPHIES

KATIE LAJINESS

abdopublishing.com

Published by Abdo Publishing, a division of ABDO, PO Box 398166, Minneapolis, Minnesota 55439.
Copyright © 2016 by Abdo Consulting Group, Inc. International copyrights reserved in all countries.
No part of this book may be reproduced in any form without written permission from the publisher.
Big Buddy Books™ is a trademark and logo of Abdo Publishing.

Printed in the United States of America, North Mankato, Minnesota.
102015
012016

Cover Photo: Chelsea Lauren/Getty Images.
Interior Photos: Associated Press (p. 23); Robb Cohen/Invision/AP (p. 15); Gregg DeGuire/Getty
    Images (p. 5); © iStockphoto.com (p. 9); Michael Ochs Archives/Getty Images (p. 17); Cindy
    Ord/Getty Images (p. 27); Chris Pizzello/Invision/AP (p. 29); Rich Polk/Getty Images (p. 13);
    Scott Roth/Invision/AP (p. 31); © Rodolfo Sassano/Alamy Stock Photo (p. 11); © Joe Stevens/
    Retna Ltd./Corbis (p. 25); Jordan Strauss/Invision/AP (p. 21); © WENN Ltd/Alamy Stock Photo/
    Alamy (p. 17); Katy Winn/Invision/AP (p. 19).

Coordinating Series Editor: Tamara L. Britton
Contributing Editor: Marcia Zappa
Graphic Design: Jenny Christensen

Library of Congress Cataloging-in-Publication Data

Lajiness, Katie, author.
  Meghan Trainor / Katie Lajiness.
     pages cm. -- (Big buddy pop biographies)
   ISBN 978-1-68078-062-8
1. Trainor, Meghan, 1993---Juvenile literature. 2. Singers--United States--Biography--
Juvenile literature. I. Title.
  ML3930.T67L35 2016
  782.42164092--dc23
   [B]
                          2015033027

CONTENTS

RISING STAR

Meghan Trainor is a talented singer, songwriter, and record **producer**. She writes catchy tunes that people can sing along to. Fans around the world love Meghan's hit songs!

DID YOU KNOW?
Meghan is known for writing cheerful songs that help women believe in themselves.

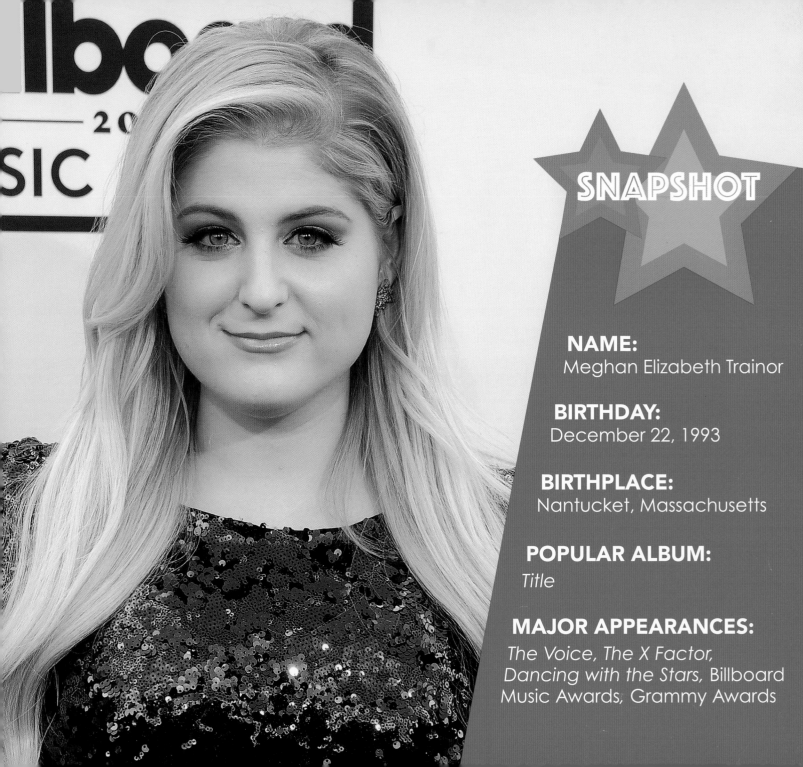

SNAPSHOT

NAME:
Meghan Elizabeth Trainor

BIRTHDAY:
December 22, 1993

BIRTHPLACE:
Nantucket, Massachusetts

POPULAR ALBUM:
Title

MAJOR APPEARANCES:
*The Voice, The X Factor,
Dancing with the Stars*, Billboard
Music Awards, Grammy Awards

FAMILY TIES

Meghan Elizabeth Trainor was born in Nantucket, Massachusetts, on December 22, 1993. Her parents are Gary and Kelli Trainor.

Meghan has two brothers named Ryan and Justin. She is the middle child.

WHERE IN THE WORLD?

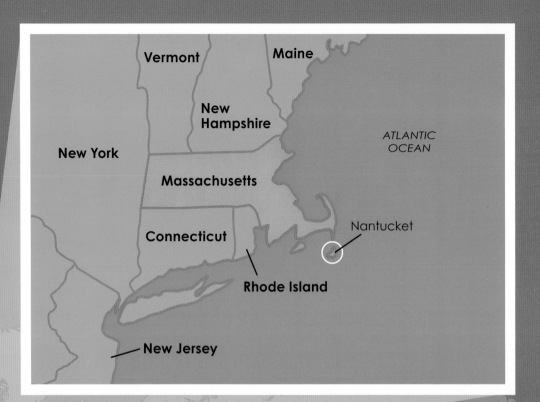

Vermont

Maine

New
Hampshire

New York

ATLANTIC
OCEAN

Massachusetts

Connecticut

Nantucket

Rhode Island

New Jersey

GROWING UP

Early on, Meghan showed an interest in making music. At six years old, she began singing in church. Meghan wrote her first song at the age of 11.

When Meghan was 12, she sang in a local band called Island Fusion. Her aunt, father, and younger brother were also part of the band. As a teenager, Meghan learned to play the **guitar**.

Meghan's father used to be a music teacher. He taught her to play the piano.

Meghan continued to write songs. In 2009 and 2010, she attended classes at the Berklee College of Music in Boston, Massachusetts. The teachers there recognized Meghan's talent right away.

Meghan attended Berklee's Five-Week Summer Performance Program. She studied pop/R&B singing in 2009 and jazz in 2010.

STARTING OUT

Meghan always dreamed big. She independently put out three albums by the time she was 18 years old.

Meghan started to win songwriting **competitions**! In 2011, she won the John Lennon Love Song Songwriting Contest.

Meghan plays the ukulele! This small, four-stringed instrument originated in Hawaii.

Finally, Meghan's hard work paid off! She signed a songwriting contract with Big Yellow Dog Music. After high school, Meghan moved to Nashville, Tennessee.

Meghan wanted to be a singer and songwriter. She wrote songs for famous singers such as Hunter Hayes and Sabrina Carpenter.

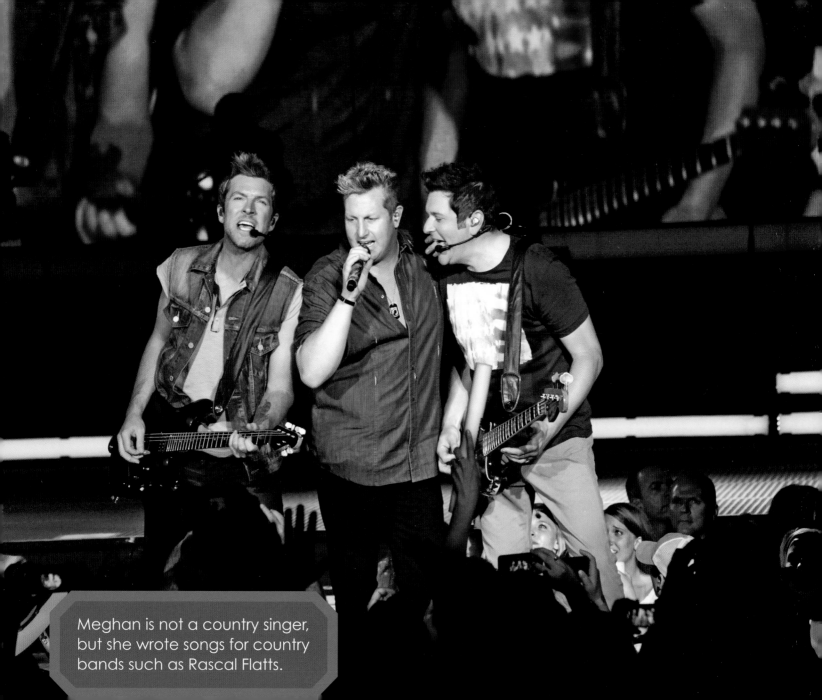

Meghan is not a country singer, but she wrote songs for country bands such as Rascal Flatts.

MIXING SOUNDS

Meghan's songwriting style is a mix of many different types of music. Some of her songs are **inspired** by popular **entertainers** from the 1950s. Meghan mixes older sounds with more current music.

Meghan's music also uses elements of soca music. This type of music is from Trinidad. Her song "Title" has a Caribbean drum beat.

Meghan enjoys listening to Frank Sinatra's music. He was a popular singer in the 1950s.

In 2014, Meghan recorded a song with Sean Kingston. Some of Sean's songs are inspired by Caribbean music.

BIG BREAK

In 2013, Meghan co-wrote the song "All About That Bass." She sent it to record **producers**. But, famous singers turned it down. Meghan believed in the song. So, she decided to sing it herself!

DID YOU KNOW ?

When Meghan wrote "All About That Bass," she didn't think it would be a hit. But, it became the number-one song on charts around the world!

Meghan co-wrote "All About That Bass" with Kevin Kadish, a writer and record producer.

When music producer L.A. Reid heard "All About That Bass," he signed Meghan to Epic Records. In 2014, the song became a huge hit!

The full *Title* album was **released** in 2015. It includes popular songs "Dear Future Husband" and "Lips Are Movin."

In 2015, Meghan and her father attended the Grammy Awards.

SINGING STAR

Title was a success! The album **debuted** at the top of the Billboard 200 Chart. Meghan traveled around the world to sing and talk about her songs.

Meghan sang on *Dancing with the Stars*, *The X Factor*, and *The Voice*. Even the characters on the television show *Glee* were singing her songs!

In 2015, Meghan sang on the television show *Sunday Night at the Palladium* in London, England.

ROLE MODEL

Meghan didn't think she looked like a **pop** star. But, she learned to accept herself for who she is. Meghan doesn't want to change to look like anyone else.

Meghan is a **role model** for young people. Her music **inspires** people all over the world to believe in themselves!

Meghan is known for her fun, fashionable clothes. She often wears stylish skirts or dresses.

OFF THE STAGE

Meghan cares about giving back to those in need. In 2015, she sang at an event for the Charlotte and Gwenyth Gray **Foundation**. This benefit helps pay for further study on an unusual illness.

To keep herself busy, Meghan also worked with FullBeauty Brands. This is a fashion line for plus-size women.

In 2015, Meghan met two young fans at a FullBeauty Brands event. She signed autographs for her fans.

BUZZ

Meghan's music continues to top the charts. In 2015, she **released** the song "Like I'm Gonna Lose You" with singer John Legend.

In 2015, Meghan was **nominated** for many **awards**. She won two Billboard Music Awards that year. With all of Meghan's success, fans are excited to see what she does next!

Meghan and John Legend sang together at the 2015 Billboard Music Awards.

GLOSSARY

award something that is given in recognition of good work or a good act.

competition (kahm-puh-TIH-shuhn) a contest between two or more persons or groups.

debut (DAY-byoo) to make a first appearance.

entertainer a person who performs for public entertainment.

foundation (faun-DAY-shuhn) an organization that controls gifts of money and services.

guitar (guh-TAHR) a stringed musical instrument played by strumming.

inspire to bring about.

nominate to name as a possible winner.

pop relating to popular music.

producer a person who oversees the making of a movie, a play, an album, or a radio or television show.

release to make available to the public.

role model a person who other people respect and try to act like.

WEBSITES

To learn more about Pop Biographies, visit **booklinks.abdopublishing.com**.
These links are routinely monitored and updated to provide
the most current information available.

INDEX